OTHER BOOKS IN THIS SERIES:

A Feast of After Dinner Jokes	A Portfolio of Business Jokes
A Binge of Diet Jokes	A Round of Golf Jokes
A Tankful of Motoring Jokes	A Romp of Naughty Jokes
A Spread of over 40s Jokes	A Triumph of over 50s Jokes
A Bouquet of Wedding Jokes	A Knockout of Sports Jokes

Published simultaneously in 1995 by Exley Publications in Great
Britain, and Exley Giftbooks in the USA.

12 11

Series Editor: Helen Exley
Editor: Elizabeth Cotton
Typeset by Delta, Watford
Printed in China

Exley Publications Ltd, 16 Chalk Hill, Watford, Herts WD19 4BG, United Kingdom.
Exley Publications LLC, 185 Main Street, Spencer, MA 01562, USA.
www.helenexleygiftbooks.com

Acknowledgements: The publishers gratefully acknowledge permission to reprint
copyright material. They would be pleased to hear from any copyright holders not
here acknowledged. Extract by Philip Oakes from the *Sunday Times* © Times
Newspapers Limited, 1969; extracts from *The Random House Book of Jokes and
Anecdotes* edited by Joe Claro reprinted by permission of Random House Inc.; extract
from *The Great Book of Funny Quotes*, by Eileen Mason reprinted by permission of
Sterling Publishing Co., Inc.

A MEGABYTE OF
COMPUTER
JOKES

CARTOONS BY
BILL STOTT

EXLEY

BLAME IT ON THE COMPUTER

"There's this company that keeps making so many errors it's thinking of buying a computer to blame them on."

F.G.

*

The computer revolution has really changed the way that we do business. Rather than bothering with elaborate excuses we just say "the computer's down."

*

"What I don't understand is, if the computer is so damn clever, how come it gets blamed for all the mistakes?"

P. MUNROE

*

"The perfect computer has just come onto the market – when it makes an error it blames another computer!"

S. J. WILCOX

*

"ANYWAY – WE'D BETTER SHUT UP – THEY'RE BACK!"

"I HAVE TO GO NOW, MY DINNER'S READY. BUT I'LL BE BACK VERY SOON..."

YOU KNOW YOUR CHILD IS COMPUTER CRAZY WHEN:

...all communication has to go through the screen.

...they takes it to bed with them.

...you catch them feeding Sonic bread and milk.

...they're disappointed when the pet mouse you give them has fur.

...they ask what sort of computer the cavemen had.

...you can't understand a word of their friends' conversation.

...they hate going to the beach because there is no power point.

...you wish you had never bought them the blasted thing in the first place....

PAM BROWN

*

PROBLEMS WITH THE PROGRAM ...

"If architects designed buildings the way programmers wrote programs, then the first woodpecker that came along would destroy civilization."

ANON

*

"New systems generate new problems."

ANON

"I'M WARNING YOU – YOU PILE OF PLASTIC – TELL ME WHAT I WANT TO KNOW OR I'LL UNPLUG YOU!"

"Someone suggested that a certain software house should have a rhinoceros as their logo. It's thick-skinned, short-sighted and charges a lot."

JAMES CRICK

*

"How many computer programmers does it take to change a lightbulb? Eight. One to analyze the problem, one to write the program, one to understand and debug the program, one to carry out the instructions and four to write the documentation."

F.G.

*

Programmer: "Computers will take over the world."
Engineer: "When they learn to wire their own plugs."

MARK SLATTERY

*

SOME ALTERNATIVE COMPUTER TERMINOLOGY

Cursor: term applied to computer users who get abusive to their machines.

Booting the Computer: applying a size 16 Doc Martens to the system box after it keeps telling you there's not enough memory to run the application.

Hard Drive: a car with no engine.

Incompatibility: any situation involving humans and computers.

Bits: the things scattered on the floor after you drop your computer down the stairs.

Hidden Files: any files you need in a hurry.

Copy Protected: any disk you *really* need to copy from.

Start Up Disk: the one disk you *always* manage to lose.

MIKE KNOWLES

*

Windows: Point, press and panic.

Virus: I don't know what's wrong either.

Hardware: The part of the computer that makes a noise when you throw it out of the window.

Motherboard: The main circuit board responsible for checking that all the other circuit boards are eating properly and wearing clean underwear.

Spreadsheet: Telling lies in columns.

D. J. FLEMING

*

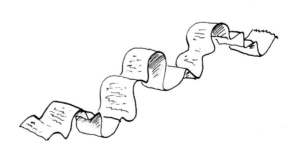

"MY GOODNESS DEIRDRE! IT SAYS IT KNOWS ABOUT US AND IT'S GOING TO TELL MY WIFE!"

Obsolete: The computer you bought three months ago.

Inadequate: The computer you bought three weeks ago.

Ideal: The computer coming on the market in three days time.

DEBBIE GREEN

*

PROGRAMMERS FROM HELL

"A doctor, a solicitor and a systems analyst were arguing about which of their professions was the most senior. The doctor claimed precedence because Adam's rib was removed and transplanted to Eve. The solicitor beat that by saying that it was law which brought order out of chaos. 'No contest,' said the analyst. 'Who do you think caused the chaos in the first place?'"

JAMES CRICK

*

"Gross incompetence is defined as '144 computer programmers'."

JAMES CRICK

*

"The personality of the programmer is reflected in the actual program. That's why computers often act like bolshy uncooperative egomaniacs with a drink problem."

D. J. FLEMING

*

"THE PROGRAM'S USER-FRIENDLY ENOUGH, BUT SOME OF THE PROGRAMMERS LEAVE SOMETHING TO BE DESIRED..."

"The computer expert invented an amazing computerized target-shooting rifle. No matter what it was pointed at, it was guaranteed to hit it.

To demonstrate the wonderful abilities of the new rifle, the computer expert challenged a champion rifle-shooter to compete against him.

On the rifle range, the champion – using an ordinary rifle – scored the highest points possible. So

"WHAT DID I TELL YOU – MY DAD KNOWS NO FEAR – HE JUST CHALLENGED ZYGOTH, LORD OF DARKNESS WITH ONLY THREE MILLION ON THE BOARD."

did the computer expert with his new rifle.

To decide the winner, two coins were tossed in the air – one for each competitor. Both coins were easily shot down.

What could be done to demonstrate that the computerized target-shooting rifle was superior to the champion with an ordinary rifle?

Suddenly, two flies buzzed overhead. 'Shoot them!' shouted a spectator.

Both rifles were soon fired and the computer expert blasted his selected fly from the sky. The champion's fly was not smashed to bits but fell, stunned to the ground.

'You missed it! I win!' said the computer expert, relieved and happy.

'Anyone can blast a fly from the sky,' replied the champion.

'But if you pick up the fly I shot and examine it closely you will observe why it still looks stunned: I made sure it will not be able to father any more children.'"

KEVIN GOLDSTEIN-JACKSON

*

"OH NO! I'M GETTING LAP-TOP THIGH!"

BUGS, VIRUSES AND OTHER AFFLICTIONS

"Computer viruses can affect humans, too. When one trashed my hard disk I felt sick for a week."

MIKE KNOWLES

∗

What did we do before computers? The same as we do now, only not so fast ... and with fewer bugs.

∗

Vernon's Laws of Computer Maintenance:

1. Never test for an error condition you don't know how to handle.
2. Software bugs are correctable only after the software is judged obsolete by the industry.

∗

"Hear about the pupil who told his teacher he was off school because he'd caught a computer virus in the Information Technology Room."

ANGUS WALKER

∗

<u>ALMOST HUMAN!</u>

"Did you hear about the computer that became a rock star after it found out it could sing? Its career plummeted when it appeared in concert unplugged."
MARK SLATTERY

*

"The advances in the newest technology have resulted in a computer that's so human it comes in late on a Monday morning!"

P. MUNROE

*

"A computer was programmed to randomly generate rock music. The programme was so successful that over a three-month period the computer wrote sixteen songs, bought a Ferrari and died of a drugs overdose."

D. J. FLEMING

*

The computer is an inadequate substitute for human intelligence, but then so are a lot of executives.

*

"THAT'S THE TROUBLE WITH THESE OLDER MODELS – IT'S

HAVING A MID-LIFE CRISIS..."

"YOU DID <u>NOT</u> BEAT ME BY FORTY-SEVEN THOUSAND!
YOU ONLY BEAT ME BY FORTY-SIX THOUSAND!"

<u>MURPHY'S LAWS OF COMPUTER GAMES:</u>

1. Never play computer games with children or teenagers, unless you enjoy being humiliated.

2. Your score of a *"shoot-'em-up"* or *"platform"* game will decrease in inverse proportion to your age.

3. If you leave your games console on the floor while playing on it, someone will always come along and jerk the power lead out during a crucial part of the game.

4. It is cheaper to keep children quiet by placing a strip of sticking plaster across their mouths than it is to buy them a computer console.

5. When children go into a computer shop they always head for the most *expensive* games.

MIKE KNOWLES

NEVER TRUST A COMPUTER!

The computer is a fantastic invention. It can calculate complex mathematical formulae, it can interact with other computers, it can analyse and evaluate data in fractions of a second, it can gather and interpret information from all over the world. It can do just about everything except get my gas bill right.

G. P. HERRICK

*"YES! AND I LOVE YOU, XR4/372, BUT PLEASE BE CAREFUL –
SOMEONE MIGHT HEAR YOU!"*

"The world's first fully computerized airliner was ready for its maiden flight without pilots or crew. The plane taxied to the loading area automatically, its doors opened automatically, the steps came out automatically. The passengers boarded the plane and took their seats.

The steps retreated automatically, the doors closed, and the airplane taxied toward the runway.

'Good afternoon, ladies and gentlemen,' a voice intoned. 'Welcome to the debut of the world's first fully computerized airliner. Everything on this aircraft is run electronically. Just sit back and relax. Nothing can go wrong … nothing can go wrong … nothing can go wrong….'"

JOE CLARO, from *The Random House Book of Jokes*

*

Breaking Down

"A friend of mine got so fed up with his personal computer breaking down that he bought a new system that was guaranteed for life. Just before the computer breaks down it will electrocute him."

KEVIN GOLDSTEIN-JACKSON

*

"Why didn't the computer pass its driving test? It crashed too often."

MARK SLATTERY

*

"The alarm on the computer beeped and a message flashed on the screen: MEMORY LOST.

The operator typed in: WHEN?

The computer screen flashed: WHEN WHAT?"

KEVIN GOLDSTEIN-JACKSON

*

"If you cross a computer with Nigel Mansell you get a system that crashes at over 200 miles an hour."

D. J. FLEMING

*

"Why are computers considered to be a step up in the business world when they're down so often?"

F.G.

*

"THE ON-BOARD COMPUTER SAYS THE CAR WON'T GO BECAUSE YOU'RE TOO ROUGH WITH IT, SIR..."

"DAD'S HOGGING THE GAMES AGAIN!"

Murphy's Laws of Computing

First Law of Systems Planning: Anything that can be changed will be changed until there is no time left to change anything.

*

Dodd's Law:
The attention span of a computer is only as long as its electrical cord.

*

Marshall's Law of Computer Management:
Technology is dominated by two types of people: those who understand what they do not manage, and those who manage what they do not understand.

ANON

*

"If Murphy had used a computer his law would probably have been lost when the machine crashed."

MIKE KNOWLES

*

"THERE HAVE BEEN LOTS OF CUT-BACKS..."

COMPUTER ERRORS

"In a few minutes a computer can make a mistake so great that it would take many men many months to equal it."

MERLE L. MEACHAM

*

"'Out of sight, out of mind' when translated by computer into Russian and back again becomes 'invisible maniac'"

ARTHUR CALDER-MARSHALL

*

"Mariner I, the Venus-bound rocket, suddenly surged off its planned course and had to be exploded … costing United States taxpayers $18.5 million. The reason: A hyphen had been left out of the flight computer program."

EILEEN MASON, from *Great Book of Funny Quotes*

*

Abandon hope, all ye who press ENTER here.

*

"People who claim that computers will make life easier for us have obviously never used one."

ANGUS WALKER

*

"With a computer we can now do a full eight hours of work in just one hour. Of course, it takes seven hours to figure out what we did."

S. K. JONES

*

"A computer is perfectly reliable until the moment you switch it on."

MIKE KNOWLES

*

"The best way to cope with today's sophisticated and highly complex software is to leave it wrapped in its box."

MIKE KNOWLES

*

A computer is a machine that can do things real fast – like get you angry.

*

"YOU'VE NEVER REALLY LIKED COMPUTERS, HAVE YOU,

GRIMSDALE?"

MEANWHILE AT THE OFFICE

"I've got this great new printer for my computer –
it can produce 250 pages in a minute. It certainly
cuts down on the paperwork!"

S. J. WILCOX

*

"Two commuters met on their way home from work.
'What was your day like?' one asked.
'Dreadful' replied the other 'the computer broke
down and we had to think for ourselves all day.'"

S. K. JONES

*

Salesman: This computer will cut your workload by 50%.
Office worker: That's great – I'll take two of them!

*

"Computing power increases as the square of the
cost. If you want to do it twice as cheaply, you have
to do it four times as fast."

ANON

"HI, RON? YOU KNOW ALL THAT STUFF ABOUT COMPUTERS
TALKING TO EACH OTHER? WELL – YOUR RS70 KEEPS CALLING
MY MT301 A GEEK."

"There are three ways of courting ruin - women, gambling and calling in technicians."

GEORGE POMPIDOU

*

"The function of a computer expert is not to be more right than the rest of us, but to be wrong for more sophisticated reasons."

JAMES CRICK

*

"WELL – I DON'T KNOW WHAT'S WRONG WITH IT – AND I'VE TRIED ALMOST EVERYTHING NOW..."

*

Syntax error: learn to type, you fool.

Printer error: when will you learn to put the paper
in before you print?

Keyboard error: pour the coffee over the plant
instead next time you have a temper tantrum.

Systems error: sack the programmer.

Disk drive failure: I'll call sales division and we'll
flog you an updated version.

MARK SLATTERY

*

I Can Remember The Days When...

... a Hard Disk was more likely to be a medical condition.

... Desk Top Publishing was a book about furniture.

... Software for Windows was a chamois leather.

... the only Business Graphics you saw in an office were on the wall of the staff toilet.

... Open Architecture was when the builder forgot to put the roof on.

... Copy Protection meant hiding your exam paper from the kid next to you.

... the only Optical Storage Device you could buy was a case for your spectacles.

... Artificial Intelligence was pretending to be clever.

... the things that needed debugging were the beds in a cheap hotel.

... a Drop Down Menu was one you accidentally knocked off the table in a restaurant."

… a Multisync Monitor turned out to be the pupil in charge of the washroom."

… the only time you got an Ink Jet was when you bought a faulty fountain pen."

MIKE KNOWLES

"THAT'S MR. PEASWADE – WE KEEP HIM ON AS A COMMERCIAL HERITAGE THING – HE'S PRE-COMPUTER."

BUILT-IN OBSOLESCENCE

"The genius of modern technology lies in making things to last fifty years and making them obsolete in three."

ANON

*

McAuley's Axiom:
If a system is of sufficient complexity, it will be built before it is designed, implemented before it is tested and outdated before it is debugged.

*

"Computers come in two varieties: the prototype and the obsolete."

ANON

*

Rolph's law of state-of-the-art technology:
If you understand it, it's obsolete.

*

"AND, WOULD YOU BELIEVE IT? IN THE BASEMENT THEY'VE GOT AN <u>ANCIENT</u> RK504! WOW, THAT BABY MUST BE <u>THREE</u> YEARS OLD!"

PLAYING THE GAME...

"Computers kept me from turning into a juvenile delinquent. Instead of getting into fights and drinking, I used to try and hack into the Pentagon and start World War Three with my Commodore 64."

ANGUS WALKER

*

"I bought PGA Golf for my PC. I don't play it – I just look for the lost balls so I can sell them at car boot sales."

ANGUS WALKER

*

"Virtual Reality games were invented to make people look silly."

MIKE KNOWLES

*

"IT WORKS EVERY TIME – I LET MY DAD PLAY WITH THE VIRTUAL REALITY HEADGEAR – SLIP IN A 'BEAT THE MUGGER' DISK AND HE TURNS OVER HIS CASH!"

"My kids are into these computer games. They call my mother-in-law an End of Level Monster!"

MIKE KNOWLES

*

The Wonders of Science

"The computer salesman was coming to the end of his demonstration of the very latest technology at the premises of C. J. Mainwairing & Son, 'And just to show you how very advanced this machine is, ask it any question – anything at all, even a personal question.'

The chief executive was sceptical. 'Okay,' he said, 'Ask it where my father is.' The salesman typed in the question and the computer began to whirr, then the answer flashed up on the screen 'Your father is sitting in a bar in Milwaukee.'

'There you are,' said the boss. 'It's wrong, my father died three years ago.'

The salesman was surprised, and hurriedly typed in, 'Where exactly is Mr. Mainwairing senior?'

The computer whirred into action and again flashed its answer on the screen. 'Mr. Mainwairing senior died three years ago, but Charlie Mainwairing's father is still sitting in that bar in Milwaukee!'"

S. J. WILCOX

*

"AND, OF COURSE – ANOTHER ATTRACTIVE FEATURE OF THE
MX7 IS THAT IT MAKES VERY FINE TOAST!"

"YES! SHE DOES HAVE REPETITIVE STRAIN INJURY – BUT ONLY
BECAUSE SHE MAKES SO MANY MISTAKES THAT SHE HAS TO KEY
IN EVERYTHING AT LEAST HALF A DOZEN TIMES!"

<u>Oops!</u>

"Computers may be unreliable, but humans are even more so...."

ANON

*

"A colleague received through the post a folder and a newsletter from the International Press Division of [a major company], breaking the news that they intend to put their business operations in the hands of a computer.

'It was only after careful analysis, rehearsal and constant checking and rechecking that it was decided that the actual computer operation would begin,' promised the letter. 'The point which cannot be over-stressed is the amount of time spent in checking the service date for each account.'

A bracing prospect, slightly dimmed by the fact that the letter was sent to the wrong address."

PHILIP OAKES, from *The Sunday Times*, 2nd February 1969

*

ME AND MY COMPUTER

"These days when a guy takes a girl to his room to show her his hardware, it usually turns out to be a 33MHz 486DX with a 120Mb hard drive and SVGA."

MIKE KNOWLES

*

"I told the wife that for all its power and sophistication, a computer was still basically a very stupid machine that can only understand two simple instructions.

'Is that so?' she said. 'Well, in that case you two should get on well together.'"

MIKE KNOWLES

*

"Using an artificial intelligence program, the first ever computer joke has been generated. It goes '01001101010101100111011'. Well *computers* think it's funny."

D. J. FLEMING

*

"THEN, WITH THE R64 MK 111 THINGS GET _REALLY_ INTERESTING..."

"A first-grade teacher was overseeing her students as they experimented with their desk computers. One boy sat staring at the screen, unsure how to get the computer going, The teacher walked over and read

"WHAT'S IT LIKE TO BE A COMPUTER?"

what was on his screen.

In her most reassuring voice, she said, 'The computer wants to know what your name is.' Then she walked over to the next child.

The boy leaned toward the screen and whispered, 'My name is David.'"

JOE CLARO, from *The Random House Book of Jokes*

"THERE'S AN ALTERNATIVE?"

"THIS NEW SYSTEM WE'VE INSTALLED IS CAPABLE OF MILLIONS
MORE MISTAKES THAN THE OLD ONE..."

To Err Is Human...

The computer is one of the great inventions of our time. There are still as many mistakes being made as ever, but now they're nobody's fault.

*

Computers are so fast now that in just a fraction of a second we can make the same stupid mistake that used to take hours before.

*

"Isn't it incredible to think that before computers were invented, we had to mess things up all on our own."

JIM FULLER

*

Computers are so versatile – not only can we work on them all day, but we can list all our errors in alphabetical order.

*

"To err is human, but to really screw things up requires a computer."

ANON

*

COMPUTER ILLITERATES

"Hear about the guy who bought a computer? He was told that opening it up would invalidate the warranty, so when he got home he refused to get it out of the box."

MIKE KNOWLES

*

"Smith couldn't understand the fuss over computer pornography. 'Why,' he exclaimed, 'surely everybody has seen a computer without its clothes on by now?'"

MARK SLATTERY

*

"It was clear that the new secretary was not used to working with computers – the computer screen had corrector fluid all over it."

KEVIN GOLDSTEIN-JACKSON

*

The major computer firms are working desperately to develop artificial intelligence. Some of the people I work with have perfected it – without the help of a computer.

*

"AND THIS IS BRADLEY. HIS DOCTOR TOLD HIM TO STAY AS FAR

AWAY AS POSSIBLE FROM COMPUTERS..."

"Technology is a queer thing. It brings you great gifts with one hand, and it stabs you in the back with the other."

C. P. SNOW

*

The world of work is intimidating. After years of college and post-graduate study plus work training, they sit you at a desk in front of this tiny little machine that's cleverer than you are."

P. MUNROE

*

If computers are supposed to be "user friendly" and "the tool of the executive" then how come we have to take classes to learn to do things their way?

*

"AH, PANGBOURNE – YOUR COMPUTER TELLS ME THAT YOU'VE BEEN THINKING BAD THINGS ABOUT THE COMPANY..."

"They sacked this guy at the office because they bought this computer that could do everything that he could do but better. Sadly, when he told his wife about it she went out and bought the same computer."

S.K.

*

Smarter Than Us!

Computers are definitely smarter than people. When's the last time you heard of six computers getting together to form a committee?

*

"BEEP, BEEP, BEEP! IS THAT ALL YOU CAN SAY?"

"ACTUALLY, NO – BUT I THINK ITS ALL YOU CAN COPE WITH..."

"A computer is only as stupid as its owner."

MIKE KNOWLES

*

"Computers could never completely replace humans. They may become capable of artificial intelligence, but they will never master real stupidity like we have."

S. J. WILCOX

*